2015
MODERN CHRISTIAN HITS
FOR UKULELE

CONTENTS

Produced by
Alfred Music
P.O. Box 10003
Van Nuys, CA 91410-0003
alfred.com

Printed in USA.

ISBN-10: 1-4706-2742-6
ISBN-13: 978-1-4706-2742-3

10,000 REASONS (BLESS THE LORD)

Words and Music by
MATT REDMAN and JONAS MYRIN

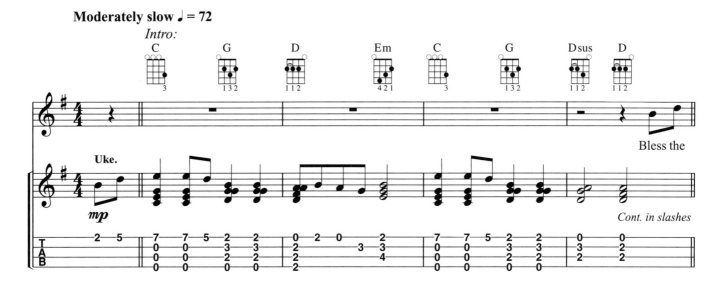

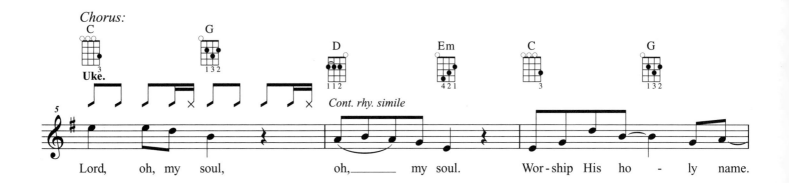

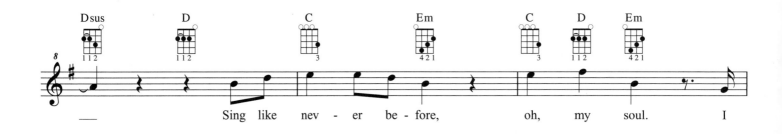

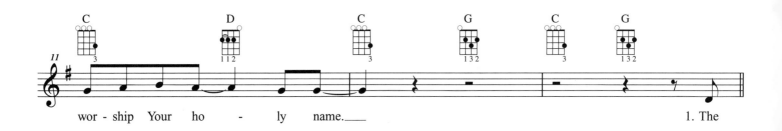

10,000 Reasons (Bless the Lord) - 4 - 1

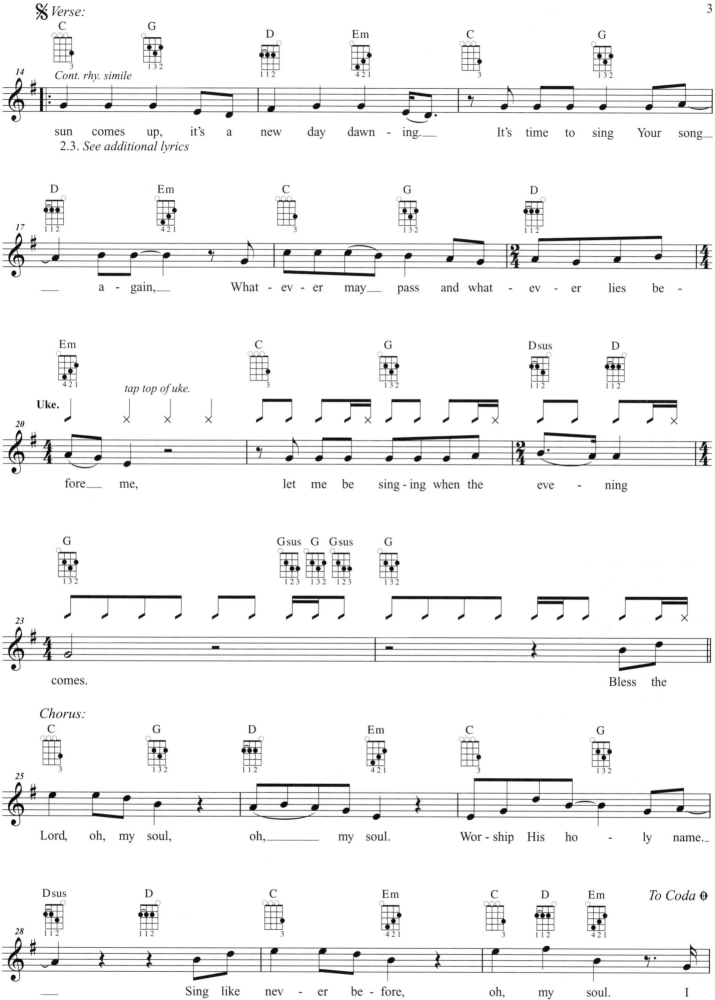

4

Verse 2:
You're rich in love and You're slow to anger.
Your name is great, and Your heart is kind.
For all Your goodness I will keep on singing
Ten thousand reasons for my heart to find.
(To Chorus:)

Verse 3:
And on that day when my strength is failing,
The end draws near and my time has come.
Still, my soul will sing Your praise unending,
Ten thousand years and then forever more.
(To Chorus:)

BLESSED BE YOUR NAME

*Tune down 1/2 step to match recording:
④ = G♭ ② = E♭
③ = C♭ ① = A♭

Words and Music by
BETH REDMAN and MATT REDMAN

*Recording sounds one half step lower than written.

Blessed Be Your Name - 4 - 1

8

Blessed Be Your Name - 4 - 4

EVERLASTING GOD

*Tune down 1/2 step to match recording:
④ = G♭   ② = E♭
③ = C♭   ① = A♭

Words and Music by
BRENTON BROWN and KEN RILEY

Moderately ♩ = 120

Verse:

Strength will rise as we wait___ up - on the Lord, wait___ up - on the Lord, we will wait

*Recording sounds a half step lower than written.

up - on the Lord. Strength will rise as we wait___ up - on the Lord, wait__

___ up - on the Lord, we will wait up - on the Lord. Our God,____ You reign__

Pre-chorus:

___ for - ev - er.___ Our hope,___ our strong_

Chorus:

___ de - liv - er - er._____ You are__ the ev-

Everlasting God - 3 - 1

-er - last - ing God,___ the ev - er - last - ing God.___ You do___

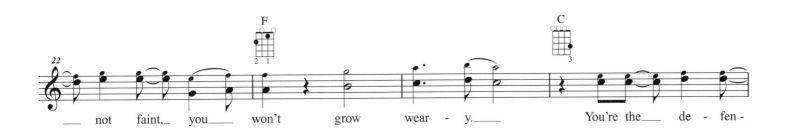

___ not faint,___ you___ won't grow wear - y.___ You're the___ de - fen -

- der of___ the weak,___ You com - fort those_ in need.___ You lift___

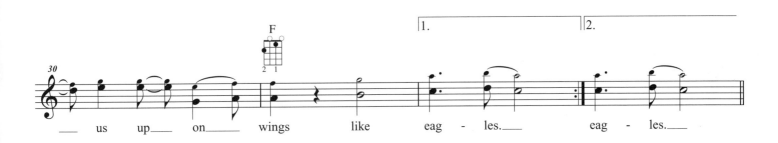

___ us up___ on wings like eag - les.___ eag - les.___

Instrumental:

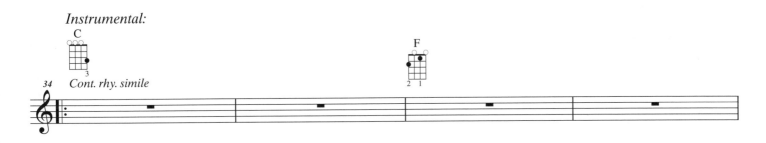

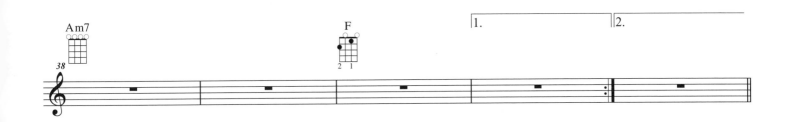

12

Refrain:

43 *Cont. rhy. simile*

Strength will rise as we wait___ up - on the Lord, wait___ up - on the Lord, we will wait

You are___ the ev - er - last - ing God,___ the ev -

46

- er - last - ing God,___ Strength will rise as we wait___ up - on the Lord, wait___

- er - last - ing God,___ the ev - er - last - ing God.___

1.2.   *Repeat ad lib.* 3.

49

___ up - on the Lord, we will wait up - on the Lord. up - on the Lord.

___ the ev - er - last - ing. - er - last - ing.

Outro:

Uke.

52 *w/spoken recitation by child (see additional lyrics)*

1.2.

3.

58

Recitation (spoken by child:)
The Lord is the everlasting God,
The creator of all the Earth,
He never grows weak or weary.
No one can measure the depths of His understanding.
He gives power to the weak, and strength to the powerless.
Even youth will become weak and tired,
And young men will fall in exhaustion.
But those who trust in the Lord will find new strength.
They will soar high on wings like eagles,
They will run and not grow weary,
They will walk and not faint.

Everlasting God - 3 - 3

GOD OF WONDERS

Words and Music by
MARC BYRD and STEVE HINDALONG

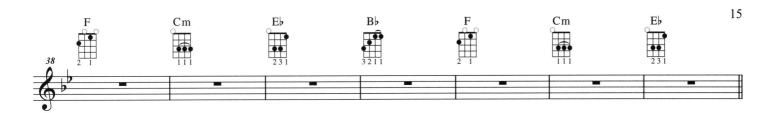

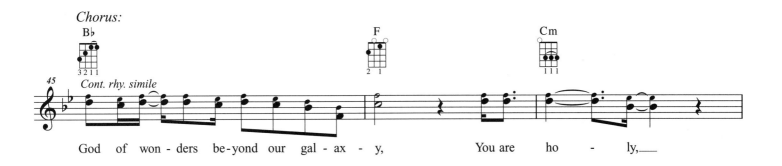

Chorus:

God of won - ders be - yond our gal - ax - y, You are ho - ly,___

ho - ly.___ The u - ni - verse_ de - clares_ Your maj - es - ty, You are

ho - ly,___ ho - ly.___ ho - ly.___

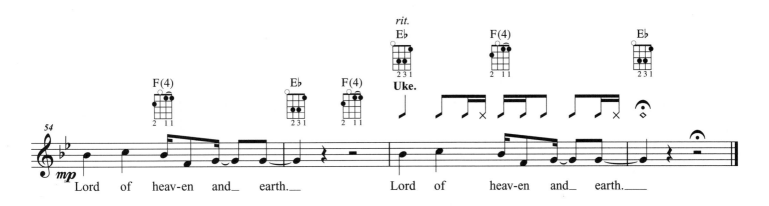

Lord of heav - en and_ earth.___ Lord of heav - en and_ earth.___

GREATER

Words and Music by
BARRY GRAUL, BART MILLARD, BEN GLOVER,
DAVID ARTHUR GARCIA, MIKE SCHEUCHZER,
NATHAN COCHRAN and ROBBY SHAFFER

Moderately, with a half-time feel ♩ = 116

Greater - 4 - 1

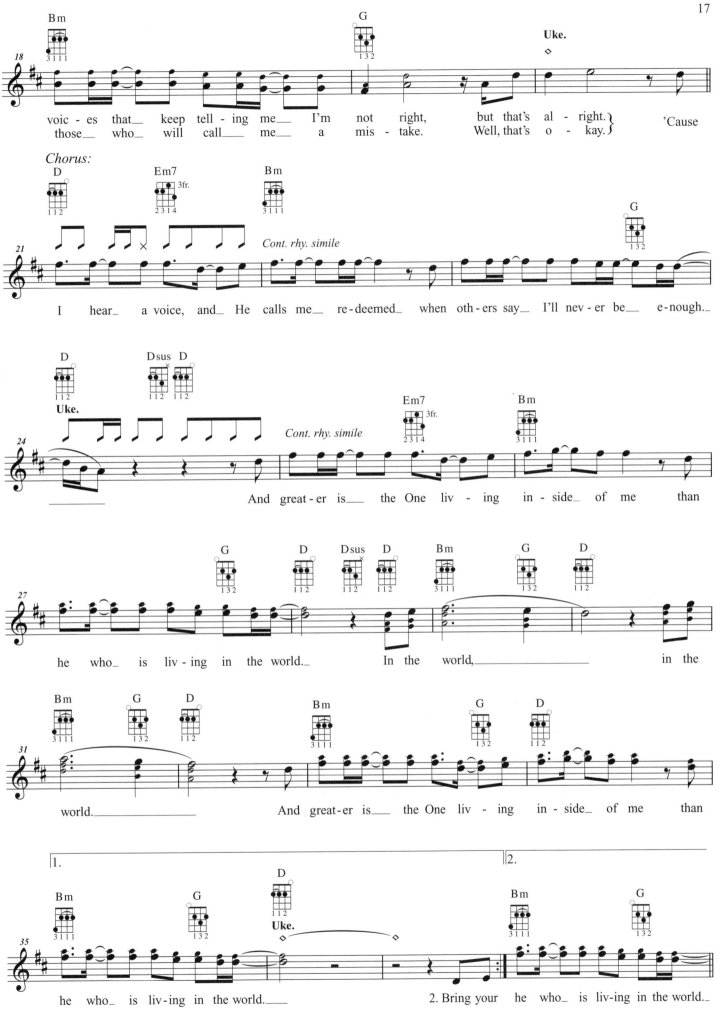

Bridge:

Oh,_____ oh._____ Oh,_____

(He's great - er, He's great - er.) Oh,_____ oh,_____

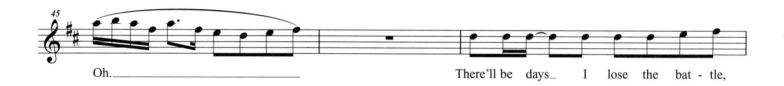

Oh._____ There'll be days_ I lose the bat - tle,

grace says_ that it does-n't mat - ter 'cause the cross_ al - read - y won the war._____ (He's great-er. He's great-er.)

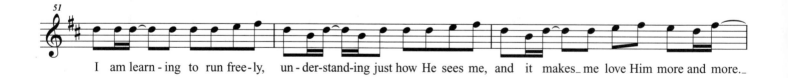

I am learn - ing to run free-ly, un - der-stand-ing just how He sees me, and it makes_ me love Him more and more._

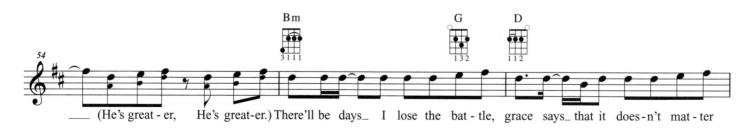

____ (He's great - er, He's great-er.) There'll be days_ I lose the bat - tle, grace says_ that it does-n't mat - ter

'cause the cross_ al-read-y won the war._____ (He's great-er. He's great-er.) I am learn-ing to run free-ly,

un-der-stand-ing just how He sees me, and it makes_me love Him more and more._ (He's great-er, He's great-er.)

Oh!_____ 'Cause he who_ is liv-ing in the world._ There'll be days_ I lose the bat-tle,

grace says_that it does-n't mat-ter 'cause the cross_ al-read-y won the war._____ (He's great-er. He's great-er.)

I am learn-ing to run free-ly, un-der-stand-ing just how He sees me, and it makes_me love Him more and more.

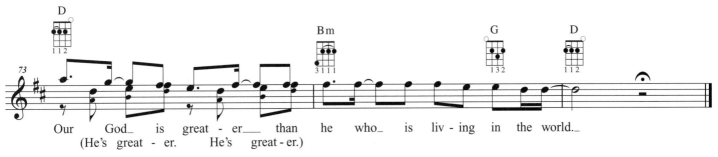

Our God_ is great-er___ than he who_ is liv-ing in the world._
(He's great-er. He's great-er.)

Greater - 4 - 4

HE KNOWS MY NAME

*To match record key, Capo I

Words and Music by
TOMMY WALKER

*Recording sounds a half step higher than written.

Spent to-day__ in a con-ver-sa-tion in the mir-ror face to face__ with some-bod-y less__ than per-fect. I would-n't choose_ me first__ if I was look-ing for__ a cham-pion. In fact, I'd un-der-stand__ if You picked ev-'ry-one__ be-fore__ me. But that's just not__ my sto-ry. True to who__ You

He Knows My Name - 3 - 1

HOLY IS THE LORD

*To match record key, Capo I

Words and Music by
CHRIS TOMLIN and LOUIE GIGLIO

Moderately ♩ = 90

*Recording sounds a half step higher than written.

Holy Is the Lord - 3 - 1

24

25

Holy Is the Lord - 3 - 3

HOW GREAT IS OUR GOD

*To match record key, Capo I

Words and Music by
JESSE REEVES, CHRIS TOMLIN and ED CASH

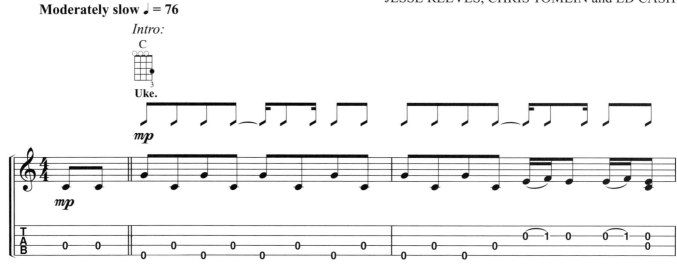

*Recording sounds a half step higher than written.

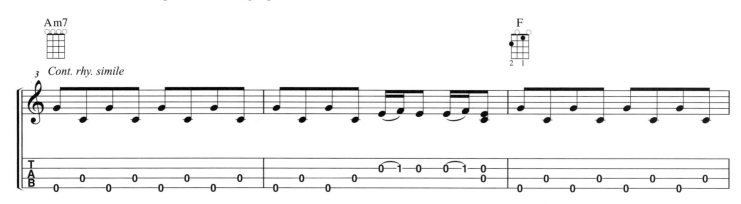

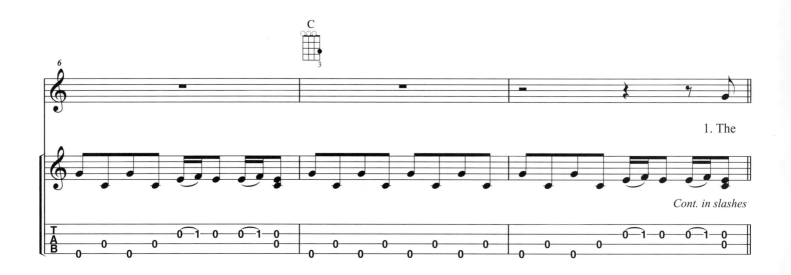

How Great Is Our God - 3 - 1

28

LEAD ME

*To match record key, Capo I

Words and Music by
CHRIS ROHMAN, JASON INGRAM
and MATT HAMMITT

Lead Me - 3 - 1

I can't._ Don't leave__ me__ hun-gry for love,_ chas - ing___ dreams. But

what a - bout us? Show me__ you're will-ing to fight,___ that I'm still__ the

love of your life. I know we__ call__ this our home,__ but I_____ still feel_

__ a - lone."_ So Fa -

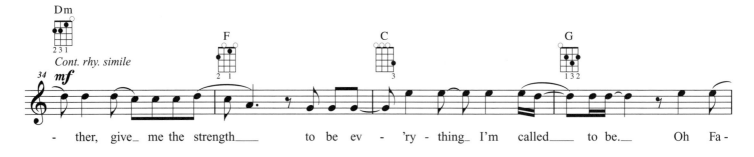

- ther, give_ me the strength___ to be ev - 'ry - thing_ I'm called__ to be._ Oh Fa -

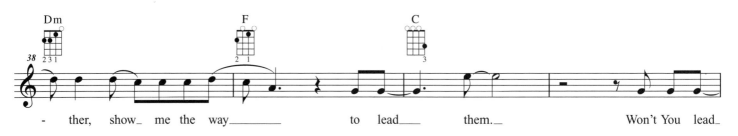

- ther, show_ me the way____ to lead__ them._ Won't You lead_

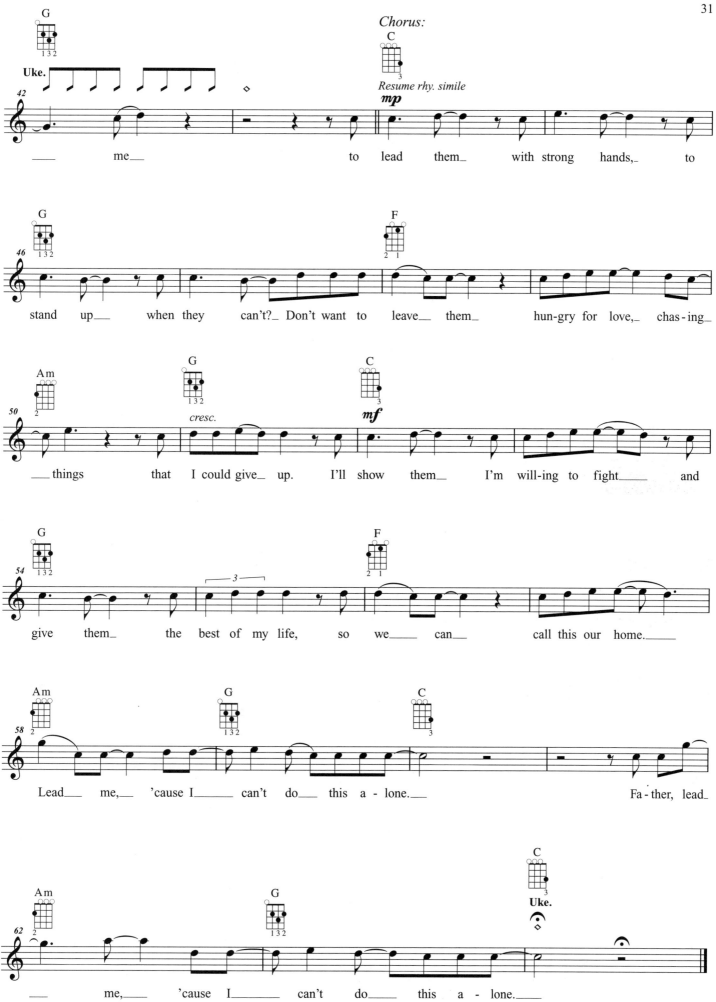

LET THE PRAISES RING

Words and Music by
LINCOLN BREWSTER

Let the Praises Ring - 4 - 1

D.S. % al Coda

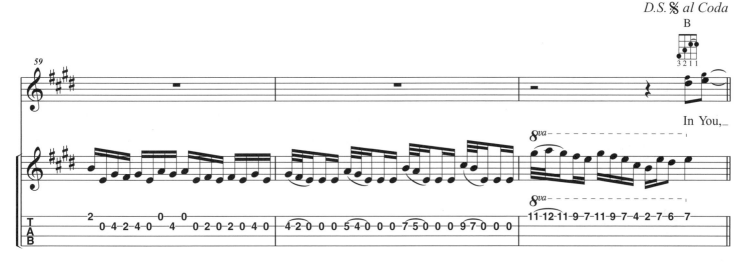

In You,__

$\oplus$ *Coda*

w/Rhy. Fig. 1 *(Uke. 2), simile (see meas. 2–9)*

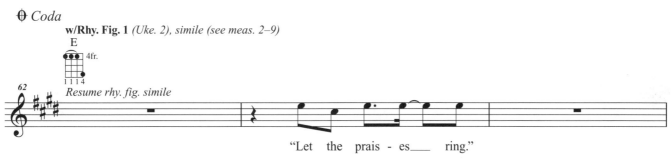

"Let   the   prais - es___   ring."

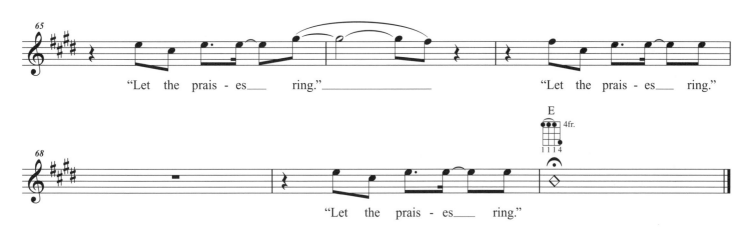

"Let   the   prais - es___   ring."_____   "Let   the   prais - es___   ring."

"Let   the   prais - es___   ring."

LORD, I NEED YOU

Words and Music by
CHRISTY NOCKELS, DANIEL CARSON, JESSE REEVES,
KRISTIAN STANFILL and MATT MAHER

____ way. When I can-not stand, I'll fall on You._

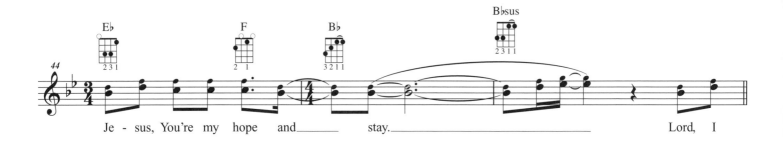

_Je - sus, You're my hope and_____ stay._____ Lord, I_

Chorus:

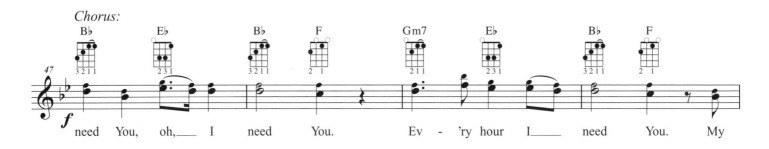

_need You, oh,___ I need You. Ev - 'ry hour I___ need You. My_

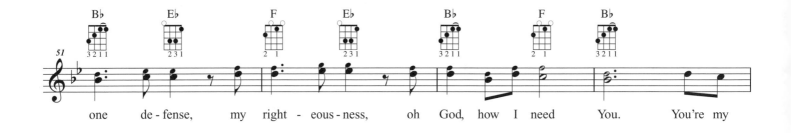

one de - fense, my right - eous - ness, oh God, how I need You. You're my

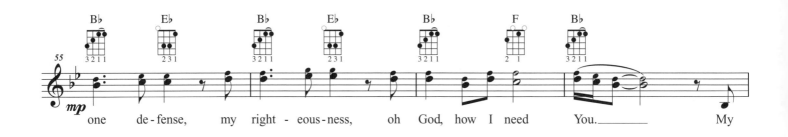

_one de - fense, my right - eous - ness, oh God, how I need You._____ My_

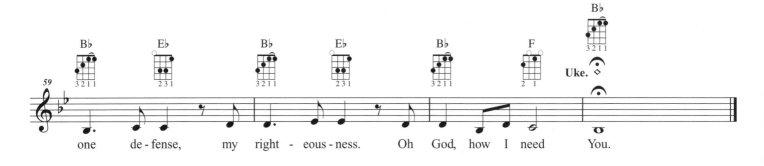

one de - fense, my right - eous - ness. Oh God, how I need You.

MADE NEW

Words and Music by
JOSIAH JAMES, LINCOLN BREWSTER
and COLBY WEDGEWORTH

Made New - 3 - 1

MULTIPLIED

Words and Music by
NATHANIEL RINEHART and WILLIAM RINEHART

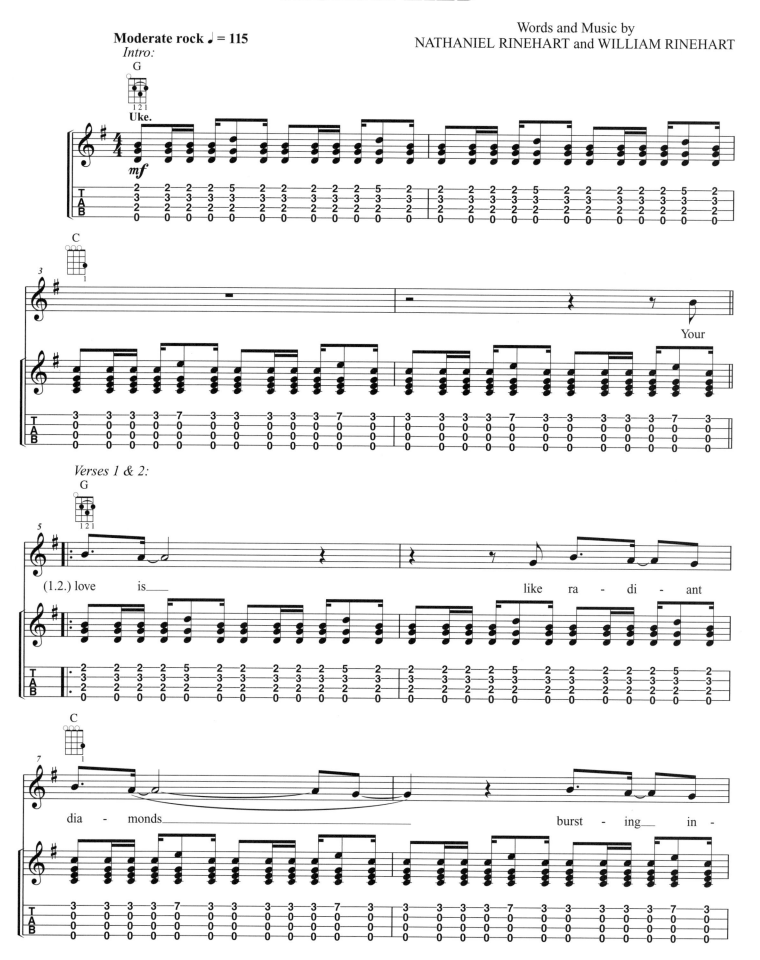

Multiplied - 4 - 1

44   *Chorus:*

Multiplied - 4 - 4

OPEN THE EYES OF MY HEART

Words and Music by
PAUL BALOCHE

Open the Eyes of My Heart - 4 - 1

Open the Eyes of My Heart - 4 - 4

OUR GOD

Words and Music by
JESSE REEVES, CHRIS TOMLIN,
MATT REDMAN and JONAS MYRIN

*Tune down 1/2 step to match recording:
④ = G♭ ② = E♭
③ = C♭ ① = A♭

Moderately ♩ = 108

*Recording sounds a half step lower than written.

Our God - 4 - 1

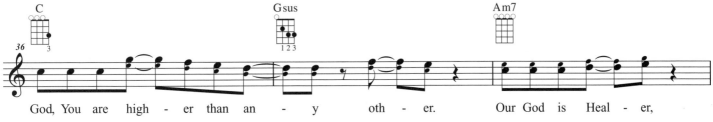

WHO AM I

*Tune down 1/2 step to match recording:
④ = G♭ ② = E♭
③ = C♭ ① = A♭

Words and Music by
MARK HALL

Moderately slow ♩ = 76

*Recording sounds a half step lower than written.

1. Who am I,___

Cont. in slashes

Verse:

(2.)_____
that the Lord of all___ the earth___ would care to know_ my name,
that the eyes that see___ my sin___ would look on me__ with love_

___ would care to feel_ my hurt.___ Who am I,___
___ and watch me rise_ a - gain.___ Who am I,___

that the Bright and Morn - ing Star___ would choose to light_ the way
that the voice that calmed___ the sea___ would call out through_ the rain_

Who Am I - 4 - 1

WHOM SHALL I FEAR
(GOD OF ANGEL ARMIES)

Moderately slow rock ♩ = 75

Words and Music by
CHRIS TOMLIN, ED CASH
and SCOTT CASH

Verses 1 & 2:

1. You hear me when I call. You are my morn - ing song.
2. You crush the en - e - my un - der - neath my feet.

Though dark - ness fills the night, it can - not hide the light._____
You are my sword and shield, though trou - bles lin - ger still._____

Whom shall I_____

1. _____ fear?   2. _____ fear?

Chorus:

I know who goes be - fore me,_____

MORE OF YOU

Words and Music by
BEN GLOVER, COLTON DIXON
and DAVID ARTHUR GARCIA

Moderate rock ♩ = 80

More of You - 3 - 1

64